Beach

By Barbara Paulding

PETER PAUPER PRESS, INC.
White Plains, New York

For my husband,
Jeffrey Hodnicki, who knows how to enjoy life

Illustrated by Martha Day Zschock

Designed by Margaret Rubiano

Copyright © 2013
Peter Pauper Press, Inc.
202 Mamaroneck Avenue
White Plains, NY 10601
All rights reserved
ISBN 978-1-4413-1254-9
Printed in China

7 6 5 4 3 2 1

Visit us at www.peterpauper.com

Life's a Beach

Introduction

There's something to be said for living on the sunny side of life. Who doesn't feel renewed after a day floating on waves and lying in the sun, perhaps indulging in an ice cream or a margarita as the sun sets into the sea? The beach relaxes and rejuvenates us, bringing home the realization that the fast lane is overrated. Life *is* better in flip flops, after all!

Whether you want to invite a bit of sunshine into your life, relive high times, or snorkel around in these pages for buried treasure, you'll find inspiration here to justify leaving a sign on your door that says—metaphorically or not—"Gone to the beach."

Keep calm and beach on!

Summer
afternoon—
to me those have
always been the
two most beautiful
words in the
English language.

Henry James

I must be a mermaid.... I have no fear of depths and a great fear of shallow living.

Anaïs Nin

Fill your
sand pail
with life's
hidden
treasures.

Live in
the sunshine,
swim the sea,
drink the
wild air.

Ralph Waldo Emerson

It's the simple
things in life that
bring us the most
pleasure—warm
sand, wispy clouds,
and the sound
of waves
and seagulls.

May the waves
kiss your feet,
the sand be your
seat, and your
friends outnumber
the stars.

Author unknown

Not all
those who
wander
are lost.

J. R. R. Tolkien

At the beach, life is different. A day moves not from hour to hour but leaps from mood to moment. We go with the currents, plan around the tides, follow the sun.

Sandy Gingras

My life is like a stroll
upon the beach,
As near to the ocean's
edge as I can go;
My tardy step its waves
sometimes o'erreach,
Sometimes I stay to let
them overflow.

Henry David Thoreau

In summer,
the song
sings itself.

William Carlos
Williams

Because there's nothing more beautiful than the way the ocean refuses to stop kissing the shoreline, no matter how many times it's sent away.

Sarah Kay

When anxious, uneasy, and bad thoughts come, I go to the sea, and the sea drowns them out with its great wide sounds.

Rainer Maria Rilke

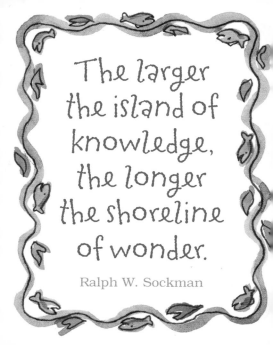

The larger
the island of
knowledge,
the longer
the shoreline
of wonder.

Ralph W. Sockman

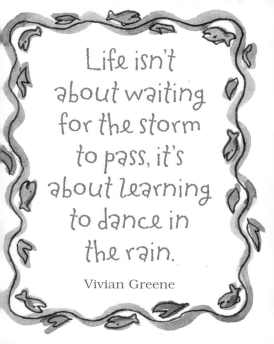

Deep summer
is when
laziness finds
respectability.

Sam Keen

And forget
not that the earth
delights to feel your
bare feet and the
winds long to play
with your hair.

Kahlil Gibran

You can't
stop the waves,
but you can
learn to surf.

Jon Kabat-Zinn

They make glorious shipwreck who are lost in seeking worlds.

Gotthold Ephraim Lessing

Throw your dreams
into space like a kite,
and you do not
know what it will
bring back, a new
life, a new friend,
a new love, or a
new country.

Anaïs Nin

Life is a tide;
float on it.
Go down with
it and go up with
it, but be
detached. Then
it is not difficult.

Prem Rawat

The seagull
sees farthest
who flies
highest.

French proverb

Every one of us is called upon, perhaps many times, to start a new life.... And onward full-tilt we go, driven in spite of everything to make good on a new shore.... Crying out: "High tide! Time to move out into the glorious debris. Time to take this life for what it is."

Barbara Kingsolver

Life is a shipwreck, but we must not forget to sing in the lifeboats.

Voltaire

After a visit
to the beach, it's
hard to believe
that we live in a
material world.

Pam Shaw

The voice of the sea speaks to the soul. The touch of the sea is sensuous, enfolding the body in its soft, close embrace.

Kate Chopin

On the
beach, you
can live
in bliss.

Dennis Wilson

Let's collect shells as we
walk down the beach.
Our treasures are many, and
all within reach.
Sand dollars, scallops, and
snails we will find,
The starfish we share,
for it's one of a kind.

Lee Nemmers

I have the world's largest collection of seashells. I keep it scattered on beaches all over the world. Maybe you've seen some of it.

Steven Wright

Every
drop in
the ocean
counts.

Yoko Ono

The waves
of the sea
help me get
back to me.

Jill Davis

The only problem with
looking for sea glass ...
is that you never look up.
You never see the view.
You never see the houses
or the ocean, because
you're afraid you'll miss
something in the sand.

Anita Shreve

Sand Castles

A mermaid hostess pours rose tea
near sand castles by the sea.
Her butterfly guests alight on cups
and sip their drink between hiccups.
As they gather on the strand
waves make poetry on the sand.
The sun paints silver on the sea
in the magical teatime jubilee.

Lee Nemmers

You can't direct the wind, but you can adjust your sails.

Beach saying

He was not
bone and feather
but a perfect idea
of freedom and
flight, limited by
nothing at all.

Richard Bach,
*Jonathan Livingston
Seagull*

It is perhaps a more fortunate destiny to have a taste for collecting shells than to be born a millionaire.

Robert Louis Stevenson

Lazy days,
beautiful nights,
beachy hair,
water fights.
Hot guys, tanned
skin, school's out,
summer's in.

Author unknown

There was something sacred about those afternoons.... The browner my skin turned, the more clearly I understood the sun truly is a god worthy of worship.... I felt him ... infuse my cells as I drifted in and out of sleep, floated on pillowy clouds of sun-induced lethargy, head spinning with idle questions.

Sol Luckman

To stand at the edge
of the sea, to sense the ebb
and flow of the tides, to feel
the breath of a mist moving
over a great salt marsh ... is
to have knowledge of things
that are as nearly eternal as
any earthly life can be.

Rachel Carson

To find a
seashell is to
discover a
world of
imagination.

Michelle Held

The
ocean is
a mighty
harmonist.

William Wordsworth

A vacation
is having
nothing to
do and all day
to do it in.

Robert Orben

Summer is the time when one sheds one's tensions with one's clothes, and the right kind of day is jeweled balm for the battered spirit. A few of those days and you can become drunk with the belief that all's right with the world.

Ada Louise Huxtable

Then followed that
beautiful season...
Summer!...Filled was the air
with a dreamy and magical
light; and the landscape
Lay as if new—
created in all the
freshness of childhood.

Henry Wadsworth
Longfellow

Let us dance in the sun, wearing wild flowers in our hair.

Susan Polis Schutz

It's only
when the tide
goes out that
you learn who's
been swimming
naked.

Warren Buffett

One doesn't discover new lands without consenting to lose sight, for a very long time, of the shore.

André Gide

You can shake
the sand out of
your shoes but
it never leaves
your soul.

Beach saying

A sailor's joys are as simple as a child's.

Bernard Moitessier

When I
forget how
talented God
is, I look to
the sea.

Whoopi Goldberg

The lowest ebb is the turn of the tide.

Henry Wadsworth
Longfellow

The sea
fires our
imagination
and rekindles
our spirit.

Wyland

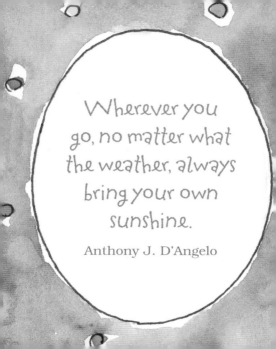

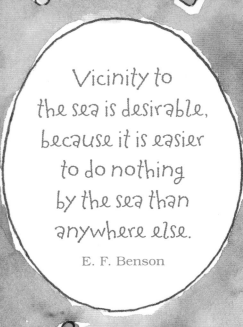

Vicinity to
the sea is desirable,
because it is easier
to do nothing
by the sea than
anywhere else.

E. F. Benson

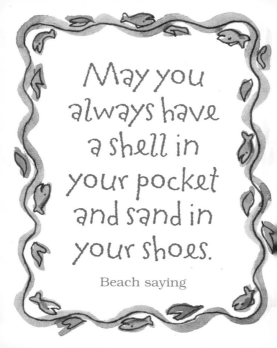

May you
always have
a shell in
your pocket
and sand in
your shoes.

Beach saying

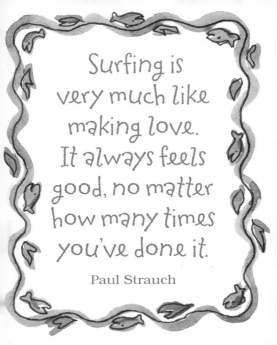

Surfing is very much like making love. It always feels good, no matter how many times you've done it.

Paul Strauch

It's hard for me to put into words why I like the beach so much. Everything about it is renewing for me, almost like therapy ... beach therapy.

Amy Dykens

Love one another
but make not a bond
of love: Let it rather
be a moving sea
between the shores
of your souls.

Kahlil Gibran

Clouds come floating into my life, no longer to carry rain or usher storm, but to add color to my sunset sky.

Rabindranath Tagore

Life is a little like a message in a bottle, to be carried by the winds and the tides.

Gene Tierney

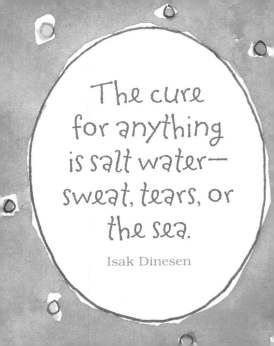

The cure
for anything
is salt water—
sweat, tears, or
the sea.

Isak Dinesen

The beach is in
our blood. Everyone
in our family
returns to the beach
instinctively, just
like the sea turtles.

Sandy Archibald

Life's better in flip flops.

Beach saying

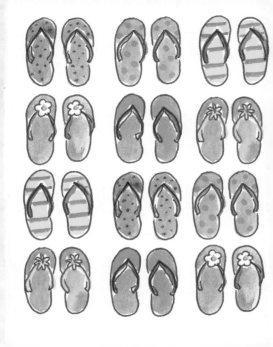

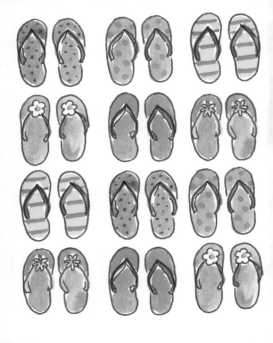